Read-About® Geography

South Dakota

By Dale-Marie Bryan

Subject Consultant
Fritz Gritzner
Distinguished Professor of Geography
South Dakota State University
Brookings, South Dakota

Reading Consultant
Cecilia Minden-Cupp, PhD
Former Director of the Language and Literacy Program
Harvard Graduate School of Education
Cambridge, Massachusetts

Children's Press®
A Division of Scholastic Inc.
New York   Toronto   London   Auckland   Sydney
Mexico City   New Delhi   Hong Kong
Danbury, Connecticut

Designer: Herman Adler Design
Photo Researcher: Caroline Anderson
The photo on the cover shows Badlands National Park in South Dakota.

Library of Congress Cataloging-in-Publication Data

Bryan, Dale-Marie, 1953–
    South Dakota / by Dale-Marie Bryan.
        p. cm. — (Rookie read-about geography)
    Includes index.
    ISBN-10: 0-516-25444-8 (lib. bdg.)   0-516-25593-2 (pbk.)
    ISBN-13: 978-0-516-25444-9 (lib. bdg.)   978-0-516-25593-4 (pbk.)
    1. South Dakota—Juvenile literature. 2. South Dakota—Geography—Juvenile
literature. I. Title. II. Series.
    F651.3.B795 2006
    917.8304'34—dc22   2005024797

Do you know how people describe South Dakota? They call it a state of "Great Faces, Great Places."

Mount Rushmore is one of South Dakota's famous places. It features carvings of the faces of four U.S. presidents.

They say this because South Dakota is filled with many interesting people and places!

South Dakota is located in the middle of the United States. It touches six other states.

Can you find South Dakota on this map?

The Chinese ring-necked
pheasant is South Dakota's
state bird.

The state flower is the pasqueflower (PASK-flau-uhr). It blooms on South Dakota's hillsides.

The Missouri River divides South Dakota in half.

Many different fish live
in the Missouri River.
The walleye is the state fish.

A cow grazes near a cabin on South Dakota's Drift Prairie.

10

Eastern South Dakota is called the Drift Prairie. This area is covered by rolling plains and low hills.

Giant sheets of ice called glaciers moved across the land thousands of years ago. These glaciers carved many lakes in eastern South Dakota.

The southeast corner of South Dakota is called the Dissected (di-SEK-tuhd) Till Plains. This area is good for farming.

Wheat, corn, and sunflowers grow in the Dissected Till Plains.

Sunflowers bloom on the Dissected Till Plains.

Some buffalo still roam South Dakota's Great Plains.

The western part of
South Dakota is called
the Great Plains. Buffalo
once roamed there.
Hunters killed many of
the buffalo in the 1800s.

Ranchers now raise
sheep and cattle on the
Great Plains.

The Black Hills rise above the Great Plains. They look black because of the many trees that grow on the mountainsides.

South Dakota's state tree
is the Black Hills spruce.

Harney Peak

Gold, silver, and copper are found in the Black Hills.

The highest spot in South Dakota is Harney Peak. It rises more than 7,200 feet (2,200 meters) in the Black Hills.

Mount Rushmore is located in the Black Hills. An artist named Gutzon Borglum carved the faces of four U.S. presidents into the mountainside.

These presidents are George Washington, Thomas Jefferson, Theodore Roosevelt, and Abraham Lincoln.

Mount Rushmore shows the faces of (left to right) George Washington, Thomas Jefferson, Theodore Roosevelt, and Abraham Lincoln.

The Crazy Horse Memorial

Artists are carving another huge image in the Black Hills. This image is of a famous Native American warrior called Crazy Horse.

The Badlands are east
of the Black Hills. Many
fossils have been found
in this area.

Fossils are the hardened
remains of plants and
animals that lived long ago.

Many interesting fossils have been found in South Dakota's Badlands.

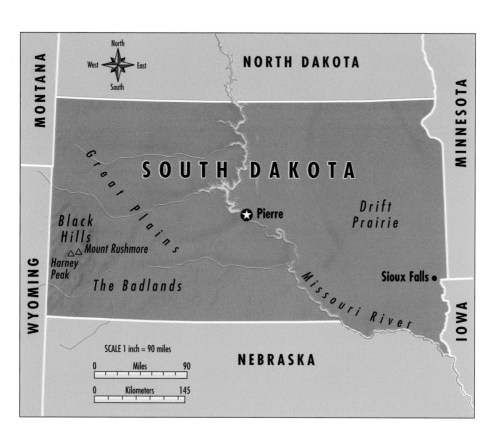

North
West · East
South

NORTH DAKOTA

MONTANA

MINNESOTA

Great Plains

SOUTH DAKOTA

*Black
Hills*
△△ Mount Rushmore
Harney
Peak

⭐ Pierre

*Drift
Prairie*

The Badlands

Missouri River

Sioux Falls ●

WYOMING

IOWA

SCALE 1 inch = 90 miles

0   Miles   90

0   Kilometers   145

NEBRASKA

Sioux Falls is the largest city in South Dakota. Pierre is the state capital.

Maybe you will visit South Dakota someday.

What faces and places would you like to see?

A family fishes in Sylvan Lake in South Dakota's Black Hills.

Words You Know

Black Hills spruce

Chinese ring-necked
pheasant

fossils

Harney Peak

Missouri River

Mount Rushmore

pasqueflower

walleye

31

Index

About the Author

Dale-Marie Bryan and her family thought Mount Rushmore was a great place to visit. She lives and farms on the high plains of Kansas.

Photo Credits

Photographs © 2007: Alamy Images/David R. Frazier: 3, 31 top right; AP/Wide World Photos/Charles Bennett: 22; Dave G. Houser/HouserStock, Inc.: 8, 31 top left; Dembinsky Photo Assoc.: 9, 31 bottom right (Gary Meszaros), 7, 31 bottom left (Bob Sisk); Masterfile/Garry Black: 13; Photo Researchers, NY: 25, 30 bottom left (Francois Gohier), 6, 30 top right (Roger Wilmshurst); Robert Fried Photography: 14, 29; South Dakota Tourism: 17, 18, 30 top left, 30 bottom right; Superstock, Inc.: 10 (Richard Cummins), 21 (Yoshio Tomii), cover, 16.

Maps by Bob Italiano.